Book 1

50 Moodboards

COLOR CONCEPTS FOR WEDDINGS

EDITORS: ANDREA WOLF & EVI HAGENLOCHER

Andrea Wolf, Immertweg 1, 51647 Gummersbach, Germany – www.andreawolfdesigns.de
Evi Hagenlocher, Hochstadenring 7, 53119 Bonn, Germany – www.project-pinpoint.com
www.colormoodboards.com, printed in Germany – ISBN 978-3-00-057447-4

PHOTO OCTAVIAPLUSKLAUS.COM

Table of Contents

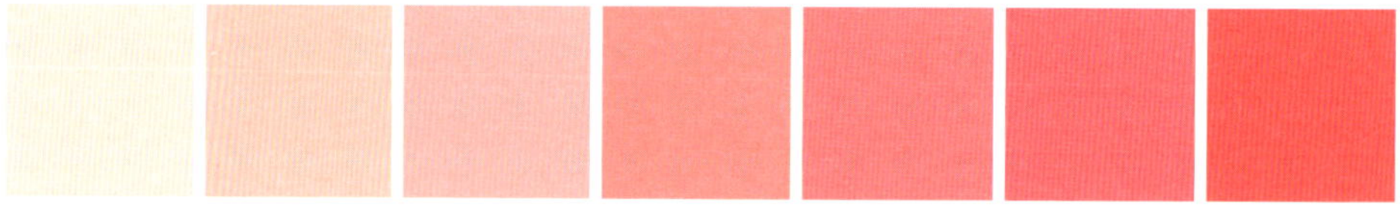

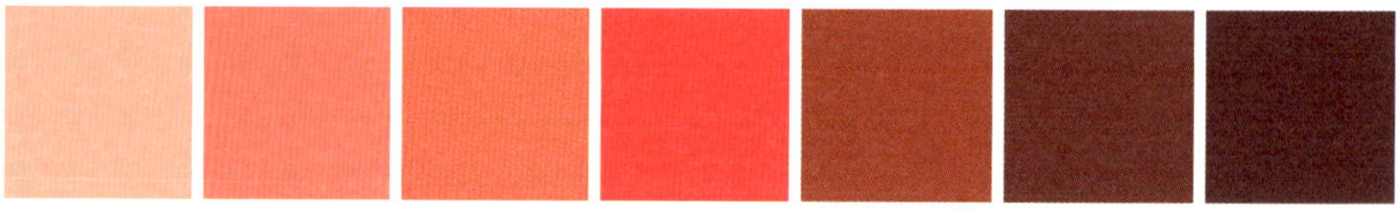

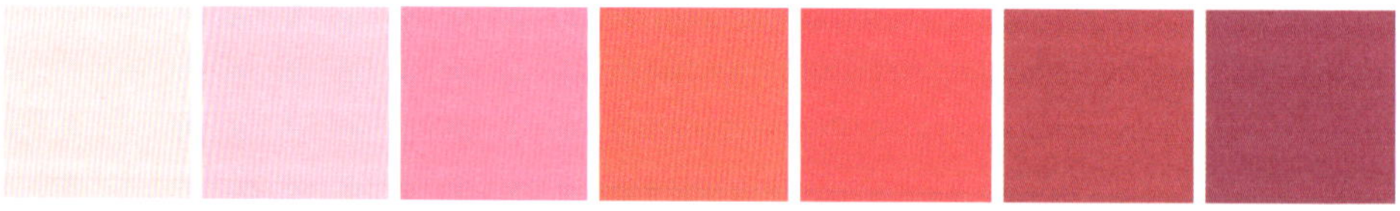

Color Palette

SHADES OF BLUE .... *page 12, 16–20, 36, 46, 54, 62, 68, 76, 88, 94*

SHADES OF TURQOUISE .... *page 20, 40, 64, 70, 74, 82, 86, 90, 96, 100, 106, 108, 110*

SHADES OF GREEN .... *page 22, 28, 32, 34, 40, 42, 50–56, 62, 64, 68, 78–84, 92, 96, 100–104, 110*

SHADES OF BROWN...................................... *page 12, 20, 32, 44, 48, 60, 64, 72, 78, 92, 98*

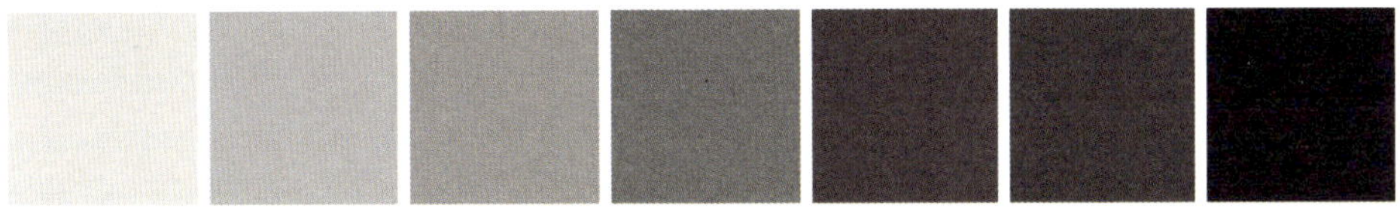

SHADES OF BLACK .... *page 12–26, 32–36, 44, 48, 50, 54, 60, 64, 70, 72, 80, 82, 96, 104–108*

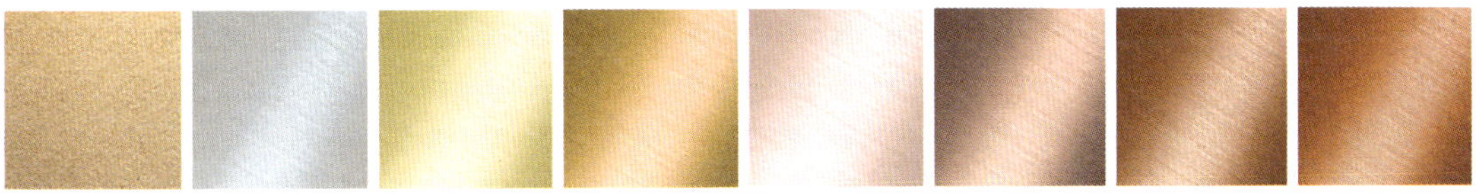

SPECIAL COLORS *page 14–18, 24, 26, 30, 34, 38–46, 50, 52, 60, 64, 68, 70, 74, 78–88, 92, 96, 98, 102, 106*

PHOTO OCTAVIAPLUSKLAUS.COM

Andrea Wolf

GRAPHIC DESIGNER, PAPER ADDICT & EDUCATOR

For more than four years the German native has been successfully designing stationery, logos and corporate designs. Within the wedding industry she is well-known for her stunning designs and high-end finishes, including foil-press, letter-press and embossing. An expert in her field, she brings a bridal couple's wedding vision to life by combining individual and unique designs with exquisite printing techniques. Since 2016 she has been successful with nuts & golden – an online store for everyday stationery items (www.nutsandgolden.de).

Die gebürtige Deutsche entwickelt seit mehr als vier Jahren erfolgreich Papeterie, Logos und Corporate Designs. In der Hochzeitsbranche zeichnet sich ihre Papeterie vor allem durch den hochwertigen Druck mit Heißfolienprägung & Letterpress aus. Mit ihrem Anspruch an Individualität, entwickelt sie für jedes ihrer Brautpaare einzigartige Papeterie. Seit 2016 betreibt Andrea Wolf erfolgreich den Papeterie-Onlineshop Nuts & Golden (www.nutsandgolden.de)

EVI'S 10 THOUGHTS ABOUT ANDREA: HARDWORKING MUM, MARKETING-EXPERT, BIG GOALS, LOVES SUSHI & WINE, EASY-GOING, INSTAPRO, TIRAMISU-HERO, LOVELY, LIKES STRIPES, FREAKING FAST

KONTAKT@ANDREAWOLFDESIGNS.DE
WWW.ANDREAWOLFDESIGNS.DE

Evi Hagenlocher

GRAPHIC & WEB DESIGNER, WEDDING ENTHUSIAST

The self-employed graphic & web designer from Austria is a well-known wedding stationery expert. In 2013, together with her sister Bettina Arnett, she founded Project-Pinpoint – an Online Store specialized in custom designed and high-end template designed wedding stationery suites. The shop is offering a variety of styles including modern, colorful, vintage, rustic and much more. For the past two years Evi has been living in Bonn, Germany, where she is working on adding new and fresh designs to her shop (www.project-pinpoint.com).

Die selbstständige Papeterie-Expertin ist eine Grafik- & Webdesignerin aus Österreich und hat im Jahr 2013 mit ihrer Schwester Bettina Arnett das Unternehmen „Project-Pinpoint" gegründet. Der Onlineshop für Hochzeitspapeterie zeichnet sich vor allem durch die umfassende Produktauswahl und Designstile aus. Seit zwei Jahren lebt und arbeitet sie in Bonn, Deutschland und entwickelt neue Designs für ihren Onlineshop (www.project-pinpoint.com).

ANDREA'S 10 THOUGHTS ABOUT EVI: PAPER-EXPERT, FOODLOVER, ALWAYS SMILING, GREAT HAIRSTYLES, SOPHISTICATED DESIGNS, LOVELY ACCENT, POSITIVE MINDSET, FUNNY, GLOBE TROTTER, SO CREATIVE

OFFICE@PROJECT-PINPOINT.COM
WWW.PROJECT-PINPOINT.COM

PHOTO OCTAVIAPLUSKLAUS.COM

Submissions

GET FEATURED

You are a wedding photographer, a wedding planner, a stationery designer or another expert in the wedding industry? You love Styled Shoots and have plenty of inspiration and a color concept to show? Great! Get featured in the next Book "50 Moodboards – Color Concepts for Weddings". Just send us your 10 best pictures with all the lovely details of a wedding as a Dropbox-Link including a list of all participating wedding services providers. Shootings which were already published in popular wedding blogs and magazines will be prefered.

Du bist Hochzeitsfotograf, Hochzeitsplaner, Papeterie-Designer oder ein anderer Experte in der Hochzeitsbranche? Du bist ein Fan von Styled Shoots und willst deine Inspiration mit Farbkonzept zeigen? Perfekt – werde Teil vom nächsten Buch "50 Moodboards – Color Concepts for Weddings". Reiche deine 10 besten Fotos mit Detailaufnahmen via Dropbox-Link und eine Liste aller mitwirkenden Dienstleister ein. Shootings, die bereits auf bekannten Hochzeitsblogs oder in Hochzeitsmagazinen veröffentlicht wurden, werden bevorzugt.

CONTACT US:
info@colormoodboards.com
www.colormoodboards.com

TO GET FEATURED:
10 best pictures via dropbox
list of wedding services providers

FOLLOW US:
instagram.com/colormoodboards
facebook.com/colormoodboards

TAG US:
@colormoodboards
#colormoodboards

There is only one happiness in life – to love and to be loved.

GEORGE SAND

PHOTO KATHLEENJOHN.DE

Moodboard I
VINTAGE FLAIR

PHOTOGRAPHY KATHIUNDCHRIS.DE, **FLOWERS, RENTAL & STYLING** SHABBYCHICEVENTS.DE,
WEDDING INVITATIONS ANDREAWOLFDESIGNS.DE, **PRINT** BUTZ-BUERKER.DE,
HAIR ANGELIKAPENNER.COM, **MAKEUP** LYDIAGERZEN.DE, **JEWELRY** TRACKULTUR.DE,
BRIDAL FASHION IAM-YOURS.DE, **CUPCAKES** DIECUPCAKERY.DE,
LOCATION SCHLOSSHOTEL-DIERSFORDT.DE, **FEATURED ON** HOCHZEITSGUIDE.COM

Amanda
Chris

Moodboard 2

VENICE ROOFTOP

PHOTOGRAPHY SUSANNEWYSOCKI.DE, **WEDDING PLANNING, DECOR & STYLING** VERENASOPHIA.DE, **CAKE & SWEETS** WIRMACHENCUPCAKES.COM, **FLOWERS** PETRAMUELLERBLUMEN.DE, **WEDDING INVITATIONS** PROJECT-PINPOINT.COM, **BRIDAL FASHION** FLAMENCO-MUNICH.DE, **DESSOUS** DASKLEIDSALZBURG.AT, **HEADPIECE** JANNIEBALTZER.COM, **HAIR & MAKEUP** MUSITOWSKI.COM, **MENSWEAR** MONSIEUR-AGNES.DE, **VIDEOGRAPHY** LILAFILM.DE, **MODELS** CHRISTIANEWERK.DE & BASTI GROSCURTH, **FEATURED IN** MARRYMAG MAGAZINE

Amore

Menu
R.S.V.P.
Vittoria Rossero
Federico Montinari

Moodboard 3

SUMMER ROMANCE

PHOTOGRAPHY NICOLEOTTOPHOTOGRAPHY.DE & DANIELAMARQUARDT.COM,
FLOWERS BLÜTENZAUBER SOLINGEN, **CUPCAKES** SUGARBIRD-CUPCAKES.DE,
WEDDING INVITATIONS ANDREAWOLFDESIGNS.DE, **PRINT** BUTZ-BUERKER.DE,
ACCESSORIES, HAIR & MAKEUP LA-CHIA.DE, **BRIDAL FASHION** IAM-YOURS.DE, **MENSWEAR** XUITS.COM,
CEREMONY OFFICIANT JEANNINE-GEBAUER.DE, **MUSIC** NEUTON.DE, **FEATURED ON** FRIEDATHERES.COM

THANKS

Moodboard 4
GOLDEN HOUR

PHOTOGRAPHY MARIEBLEYER.COM, **WEDDING PLANNING** VENUS-WEDDINGS.COM, **DECOR & STYLING** DEKO-RAUM.AT, **WEDDING INVITATIONS** PROJECT-PINPOINT.COM, **CAKE & SWEET TABLE** CAKE-SHOP.AT, **BRIDAL FASHION** SALONDIVA.SK, **HAIR & MAKEUP** FEENGLEICH-MAKEUP.COM, **JEWELRY** EDITAROSENROT.COM, **LOCATION** STRUDLHOF.AT & PALAISLIECHTENSTEIN.COM, **FEATURED IN** BRAUT MAGAZINE

Thank you
10/12/

Happily ever after
Save the Date
October 12 2014
Katherine and Johnson
Charlotte Welsh
Katherine and Johnson
would like to invite you
to celebrate their marriage
on October 12 2014 at four o'clock
at Belvedere Castle
Make a wish
Thank you

Menu

Once upon a time

Moodboard 5
OCEAN BREEZE

PHOTOGRAPHY SANDRAHUETZEN.DE, **FLOWERS & STYLING** MELANIE-NOORMANN.DE,
BRIDAL FASHION KISUI.DE, **MENSWEAR** HERRVONEDEN.COM, **CAKE** GRETARMARLENE.DE,
HAIR FRAUDEBUS.DE, **MAKEUP** KRISTINA AILEEN ROSSKAMP,
WEDDING INVITATIONS ANDREAWOLFDESIGNS.DE, **CEREMONY OFFICIANT** GLUECKSVERBREITER.DE,
LOCATION SKITERRASSEN.DE, **FEATURED ON** FRIEDATHERES.COM

Wedding

Moodboard 6

SUNNY SIDE

PHOTOGRAPHY MARIEBLEYER.COM, **WEDDING PLANNING** THE-PERFECT-DAY.AT, **DECOR & STYLING** HEYDAY-VIENNA.COM, **FLOWERS** EVELYNKUEHR.COM, **CAKE & SWEET TABLE** KUCHENMITSTIL.AT, **WEDDING INVITATIONS** PROJECT-PINPOINT.COM, **STORY** FACEBOOK/SCHOENERGEIST, **BRIDAL FASHION** HEYDAY-VIENNA.COM, **HAIR & MAKEUP** FACEBOOK/A.CONDOPOULOS, **WEDDING RINGS** ROSAMARLENE.DE, **JEWELRY** EDITAROSENROT.COM, **VIDEOGRAPHY** CASETTI.AT, **LOCATION** DIETRAEUMEREI.AT, **MODELS** HELENE & ALJOSCHA, **FEATURED IN** BRAUT MAGAZINE

Liebe fließt
HONIG vom Bio-Imker

WEDDING
PARTY

Menü
Marie & Max

sauer macht lustig
sauer macht lustig

Moodboard 7
MODERN LOFT

PHOTOGRAPHY WEDDING-YOUANDME.COM,
WEDDING PLANNING & STYLING WEDS4U.DE,
BRIDAL FASHION 123BRAUT.DE, **HAIR & MAKEUP** DOMINIKABRONNER.COM,
WEDDING INVITATIONS ANDREAWOLFDESIGNS.DE, **PRINT** BUTZ-BUERKER.DE,
CAKE & CATERING MASTERCLASS-CAKE.DE, **FEATURED ON** BRAUT.DE

Sarah & Chris
BRENDER
WINTER
SAMSTAG
26
MÄRZ
THE IVORY CLUB, FRANKFURT

Moodboard 8

ITALIAN ROMANCE

PHOTOGRAPHY OCTAVIAPLUSKLAUS.COM, **WEDDING PLANNING** CONAMORE.IT, **FLOWERS** JARDINDIVERS.IT, **WEDDING INVITATIONS** PROJECT-PINPOINT.COM, **CALLIGRAPHY LOVELETTER** JEANNETTEMOKOSCH.COM, **BRIDAL FASHION** LIGHTANDLACE.DE, **HAIR & MAKEUP** ARMILLABEAUTY.COM, **JEWELRY** LA-CHIA.DE, **GROOM'S ACCESSORIES** BEWOODEN.DE, **CAR RENTAL** NOLEGGIOCHIANTI500.IT, **MUSIC** NEOMARKS.DE, **LOCATION** MANGIACANE.COM, **FEATURED IN** BRAUT MAGAZINE

Sophie and Alessandro
Menu
Sophie
Alessandro

to come into bloom
planted on arid ground
we took our roots
to melt together,
shared the water drops
we've found,
have grown in love
stronger and better

Moodboard 9
SPRING PASTELS

PHOTOGRAPHY JULIABASMANN-PHOTOGRAPHY.DE, **FLOWERS & STYLING** STIELUNDBLUETE-GRAFENBERG.DE, **CAKE & SWEET TABLE** CAKESTYLING.DE, **HAIR & MAKEUP** PATRICIAKRANICH.DE, **BRIDAL FASHION** SINAFISCHERDESIGN.DE, **MENSWEAR** HUGO BOSS, **WEDDING INVITATIONS** ANDREAWOLFDESIGNS.DE, **PRINT** BUTZ-BUERKER.DE, **JEWELRY** FINGERGLUECK.DE, **LOCATION** GOURMETBERNER.DE, **FEATURED ON** HOCHZEITSWAHN.DE

Menü

Moodboard 10

SHADES OF PURPLE

PHOTOGRAPHY POURTOIPHOTOGRAPHIE.COM, **WEDDING PLANNING** JAVONHERZEN.DE, **CAKE & SWEET TABLE** SUESS-UND-SALZIG.DE, **COOKIE STAMP** DEIN-KEKSSTEMPEL.DE, **FLOWERS** STRAUCHDIEBIN.DE, **WEDDING INVITATIONS** PROJECT-PINPOINT.COM, **BRIDAL FASHION** BRAUTATELIER-TARA.DE, **HAIR & MAKEUP** STILETT-BOUTIQUE.EU, **DJ** SUITE219.DE, **LOCATION & CATERING** TRESS-GASTRONOMIE.DE

Sandra
&
Thomas
SAMSTAG
15
HERZLICHE EINLADUNG
ZU UNSERER HOCHZEIT
ST
85
Anfahrt
ZWIEFALTER MÜNSTER
SCHLOSS EHRENFELS
FLAIR HOTEL HIRSCH
SCHLOSS EHRENFELS
FLAIR HOTEL HIRSCH
ZWIEFALTER MÜNSTER

Moodboard II

BOHEMIAN WOODS

PHOTOGRAPHY ELENA-ENGELS.DE, **VIDEOGRAPHY** FARINA-KIRMSE.DE,
FLOWERS + STYLING SHABBYCHICEVENTS.DE, **RENTAL** NIMMPLATZ.COM,
CAKE PENNYCAKES.DE, **HAIR & MAKEUP** WEDDINGSTYLE BY CICEK,
WEDDING INVITATIONS ANDREAWOLFDESIGNS.DE, **PRINT** BUTZ-BUERKER.DE,
FEATURED IN MARRYMAG MAGAZINE

LIMO BAR

Moodboard 12

LOVE IS LOVE

PHOTOGRAPHY SIEGRIDCAIN.COM, **DECOR & STYLING** INALAVIE.COM,
FLOWERS BLUETENSTAND.AT, **CAKE & SWEET TABLE** CAKECOUTURE.AT,
WEDDING INVITATIONS PROJECT-PINPOINT.COM, **BRIDAL FASHION** DASKLEIDSALZBURG.AT,
HAIR & MAKEUP MAKE-ME-UP.AT, **JEWELRY** SCHMUCKGESTALTUNG-EDER.AT,
MODELS MELANIE & JUDITH, **FEATURED IN** MARRYMAG MAGAZINE

THEODOR
SAVE THE DATE
15 08 15
Hanna & Sophie
HANNA & SOPHIE DENKEN AN DICH!
WIR BITTEN UM ANTWORT BIS
15 06 15
GEMEINSAM MIT UNSEREN ELTERN LADEN WIR EUCH GANZ HERZLICH ZU UNSERER HOCHZEIT AM 15.AUGUST 2015 UM 14 UHR IM GUWE
Hanna & Sophie
DANKE

MENÜ
15/08/15
MONDSEEFISCH
MILCHKALB
SPARGELRISOTTO
SFOLIATA
SWEET TABLE

DANKE
15 08 15
Hanna & Sophie

Moodboard 13

WINDY WALKS

PHOTOGRAPHY NICOLEOTTOPHOTOGRAPHY.DE & DANIELAMARQUARDT.COM,
FLOWERS BLÜTENZAUBER SOLINGEN, **WEDDING INVITATIONS** ANDREAWOLFDESIGNS.DE,
BRIDAL FASHION VICTORIARUESCHE.DE, **MENSWEAR** HERRENBUDE.DE,
HAIR & MAKEUP DOMINIKABRONNER.COM, **ACCESSORIES** LA-CHIA.DE, **JEWELRY** TRAGKULTUR.DE,
CUPCAKES MADAMEMIAMMIAM.DE, **CEREMONY OFFICIANT** DIETRAUUNG.DE, **FEATURED ON** HOCHZEITSWAHN.DE

SONG OF SALOMON 3:4
I have found the one whom my soul loves

Moodboard 14

BRIAR ROSE

PHOTOGRAPHY MARIEBLEYER.COM, **WEDDING PLANNING** THE-PERFECT-DAY.AT, **DECOR & STYLING** INALAVIE.COM, **CAKE & SWEET TABLE** KUCHENMITSTIL.AT, **FLOWERS** BLAUERBAUERNHOF.AT, **WEDDING INVITATIONS** PROJECT-PINPOINT.COM, **STORY** FACEBOOK/SCHOENERGEIST, **BRIDAL FASHION** HEYDAY-VIENNA.COM, **HAIR & MAKEUP** GILBIRD.AT, **JEWELRY** EDITAROSENROT.COM, **DECOR & STYLING SUPPLIES** WYHNALEK.COM, **VIDEOGRAPHY** CASETTI.AT, **LOCATION** GRAFENEGG.COM, **MODELS** MARIE-THERESE KATHARINA & GEORG, **FEATURED IN** BRAUT MAGAZINE

Menü
Juni

Menü
KÖNIGLICH SPEISEN
HOCHZEITSSUPPE

Moodboard 15

FLORAL FINESSE

PHOTOGRAPHY ELENA-ENGELS.DE, **VIDEOGRAPHY** FARINA-KIRMSE.DE,
FLOWERS, STYLING & RENTAL SHABBYCHICEVENTS.DE,
BRIDAL FASHION IAM-YOURS.DE, **HAIR & MAKEUP** DOMINIKABRONNER.COM,
WEDDING INVITATIONS ANDREAWOLFDESIGNS.DE, **PRINT** BUTZ-BUERKER.DE,
CEREMONY OFFICIANT DIETRAUUNG.DE, **LOCATION** DOCKONE.DE, **FEATURED IN** HOCHZEITSWAHN MAGAZINE

Violette Gold
Tom Winters
Antwort
An
Frankfurter Str. 188
34121 Kassel
Menü
Save the Date
Violette Gold
Tom Winters

Wir heiraten!
Violette Gold
und
Tom Winters
15. Mai 2016

Moodboard 16

NEON EXPLOSION

PHOTOGRAPHY WEDDINGPILOTS.COM, **WEDDING PLANNING** JULIANE BACH, **CAKE & SWEET TABLE** SUESS-UND-SALZIG.DE, **FLOWERS** DIE-KATHE.DE, **WEDDING INVITATIONS** PROJECT-PINPOINT.COM, **BRIDAL FASHION/SKIRT** NONI-MODE.DE, **BRIDAL FASHION/DRESS** BRAUTATELIER-TARA.DE, AMBACHERVIDIC, **HAIR & MAKEUP** LONA-STYLING.DE, **MENSWEAR** MRASH.DE, **GROOM'S ACCESSORIES** WHITEMONKEY.DESIGN, **JEWELRY** BKING.DE, **WHISKYBAR** WHISKYANDMORE.COM, **LOCATION** DESIGNOFFICES.DE, STUTTGART-MITTE, **FEATURED IN** MARRYMAG MAGAZINE

THEO
TISCH 2

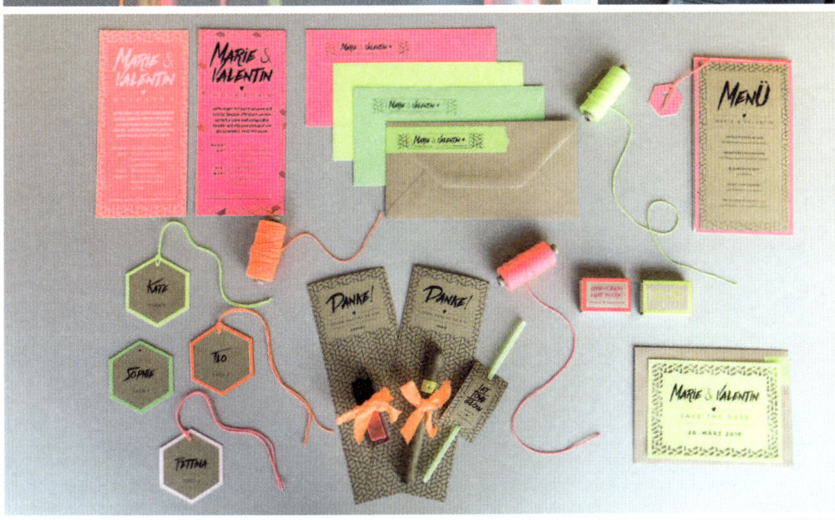
Marie & Valentin
Menü
Danke!
Danke!
Marie & Valentin
Save the date

SAVE THE

Moodboard 17

GREAT GATSBY

PHOTOGRAPHY ELENA-ENGELS.DE, **VIDEOGRAPHY** FARINA-KIRMSE.DE,
FLOWERS & STYLING SHABBYCHICEVENTS.DE, **WEDDING INVITATIONS** ANDREAWOLFDESIGNS.DE,
BRIDAL FASHION VICTORIARUESCHE.DE, **MENSWEAR** STRODELUNDJAEGER.DE,
HAIR & MAKEUP MASKENRAUM.DE, **ACCESORIES** LA-CHIA.DE, **CUPCAKES** DIECUPCAKERY.DE,
RENTAL NIMMPLATZ.COM, **LOCATION** DOCKONE.DE, **FEATURED IN** HOCHZEITSWAHN MAGAZINE

Menü
Frikassee vom falschen Kapaun mit Reis
Dessertbuffet „Surprise“

We are getting married!
Charlotte Steiner
und Oliver Keaton
Save the Date
Charlotte & Oliver

Moodboard 18
LOVELY TEA PARTY

PHOTOGRAPHY KATHARINASCHNEE.COM, **TEAM** HERZENSANGELEGENHEITEN.KOELN, **CAKES & SWEET TABLE** PENNYCAKES.DE, **FLOWERS** FLORISTIKLOUNGE.COM, **WEDDING INVITATIONS** PROJECT-PINPOINT.COM, **BRIDAL FASHION** EVASCHOLZ.COM, **HAIR & MAKEUP** DOMINIKABRONNER.COM, **CAKETOPPER** DRAHTLIEBE.COM, **RENTAL/DISHES** LIESCHENUNDRUTH.DE, **FEATURED IN** BRAUT MAGAZINE

TEA
Party

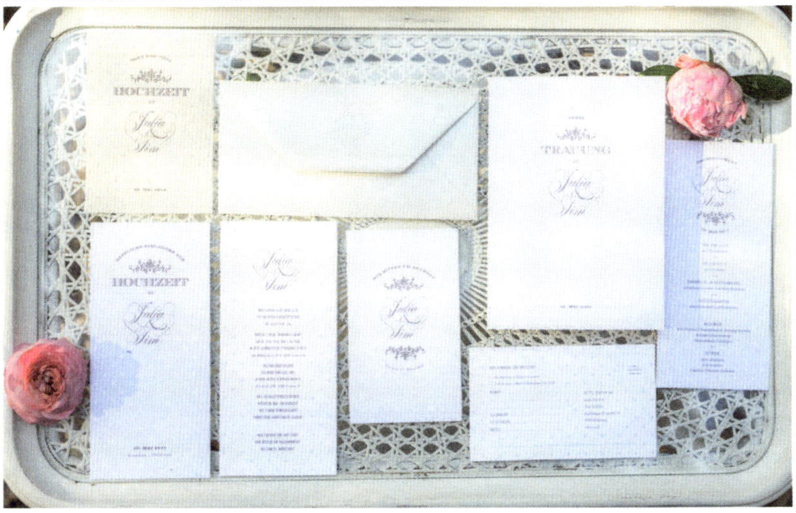
HOCHZEIT
TRAUUNG
HOCHZEIT

Moodboard 19
WHITE ON WHITE

PHOTOGRAPHY ELENA-ENGELS.DE,
FLOWERS, STYLING & RENTAL SHABBYCHICEVENTS.DE,
HAIR & MAKEUP DOMINIKABRONNER.COM,
BRIDAL FASHION IAM-YOURS.DE,
CAKE ZARTSUESS.DE, **LOCATION** FLORA KÖLN

Moodboard 20
FIELD OF FLOWERS

PHOTOGRAPHY LINSE2.AT, **DECOR & STYLING** INALAVIE.COM,
CAKE & SWEETS CAKE-SHOP.AT, **FLOWERS** BLUMENRAUMGESTALTUNG.COM,
WEDDING INVITATIONS PROJECT-PINPOINT.COM,
BRIDAL FASHION & MENSWEAR FREIWILD-DESIGN.AT,
HAIR & MAKEUP GILBIRD.AT

HAPPILY
ever after
STARTS HERE

Wir heiraten!
Pia & Emil

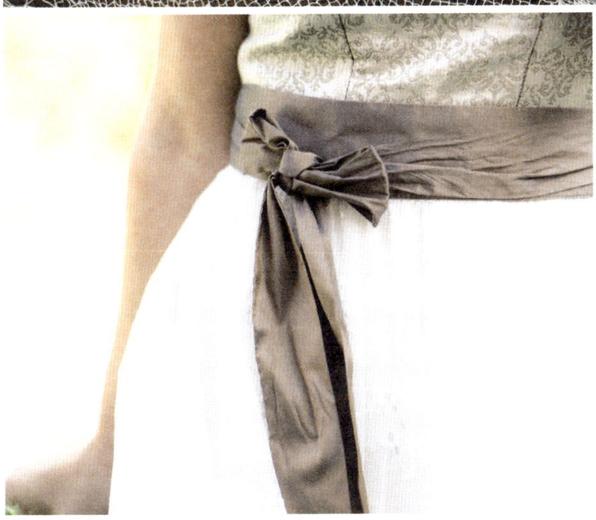

Moodboard 21

COPPER CRUSH

PHOTOGRAPHY & VIDEOGRAPHY OCTAVIAPLUSKLAUS.COM, **WEDDING PLANNING** FACTSANDFEELINGS.DE, **WEDDING INVITATIONS** ANDREAWOLFDESIGNS.DE, **PRINT** BUTZ-BUERKER.DE, **HAIR & MAKEUP** DOMINIKABRONNER.COM, **BRIDAL FASHION** VICTORIARUESCHE.DE, **MENSWEAR** MONSIEUR-ADNES.DE, **RENTAL** NIMMPLATZ.COM, **FLOWERS** GOLDREGEN-FLORALDESIGN.DE, **ACCESSORIES** JANNIEBALTZER.COM, **MUSIC** NEOMARKS.DE, **LOCATION** SCHLOSSHOTEL-DIERSFORDT.DE, **FEATURED ON** HOCHZEITSGUIDE.COM

Save the Date
Ninth December
Linda and David
Enjoy our feast

Moodboard 22
SEVENTH HEAVEN

PHOTOGRAPHY KATJAHEIL.DE, **DECOR & STYLING** FRAEULEIN-K-SAGT-JA.DE,
FLOWERS FLORISTIK-HANDWERK.DE, **WEDDING INVITATIONS** PROJECT-PINPOINT.COM,
FAVORS & GIFTS SCHOENERTAGNOCH.BLOGSPOT.IT, **BRIDAL FASHION** KISUI.DE,
HAIR & MAKEUP SCHMINKRAUM.COM, **LOCATION** VON-WINNING.DE,
MODEL FACEBOOK/SARAH.JEANNINE, **FEATURED IN** FRAEULEIN-K-SAGT-JA.DE

Menü
Menü
Amelie & Jannich

Moodboard 23
ROMANTIC HILLS

PHOTOGRAPHY JULIABASMANN-PHOTOGRAPHY.DE & NELLIMAYER.DE, **BRIDAL FASHION** TIANVANTASTIQUE.DE, **FLOWERS** WELT-DER-ROSALIE.DE & CLAUDIAREITINGER.DE, **DECOR** KÄTHES-LÄDCHEN.AT, **WEDDING INVITATIONS** ANDREAWOLFDESIGNS.DE, **PRINT** BUTZ-BUERKER.DE, **HAIR & MAKEUP** DESIREE-RENAUD.DE, **COOKIES** RICHTIG-SUESS.DE, **SHOES** SCHUHNIQUE.DE, **JEWELRY** FINGERGLUECK.DE, **ACCESSORIES** WIESN-TASCHERL.DE, **FEATURED IN** WEDDINGSTYLE MAGAZINE

Tisch
2
Menü
SOPHIA

Moodboard 24

RUSTIC AUTUMN

PHOTOGRAPHY B-PICTURES.AT,
WEDDING PLANNING, DECOR & STYLING BRAUTZAUBER.AT,
FLOWERS EVELYNKUEHR.COM,
WEDDING INVITATIONS PROJECT-PINPOINT.COM,
FEATURED IN BRAUT MAGAZINE

Best
DAY

THERESA UND EDUARD
Menü
TAFELSPITZSULZCHEN
SCHAUMSUPPE VON WIESENKRAUTERN
BLAUBEERSORBET
IN KRAUTERN GEBRATENES FILET VOM ZANDER
VARIATION VON DER VALROHNA SCHOKOLADE

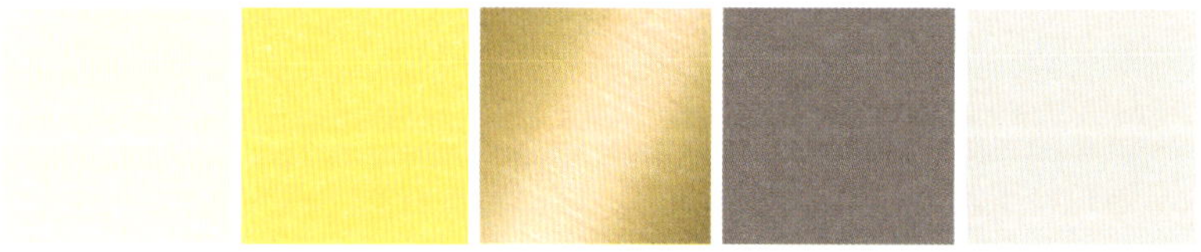

Moodboard 25
COUNTRY CHARM

PHOTOGRAPHY STEFANIENEVERSLEEPS.COM,
FLOWERS, STYLING & RENTAL SHABBYCHICEVENTS.DE,
BRIDAL FASHION KISUI.DE, **HAIR & MAKEUP** DOMINIKABRONNER.COM,
WEDDING INVITATIONS ANDREAWOLFDESIGNS.DE, **PRINT** BUTZ-BUERKER.DE,
WEDDING PLANNING SCHLIPSUNDSCHLEIER.DE, **LOCATION** HOTEL-AHE.DE, **FEATURED ON** HOCHZEITSWAHN.DE

3

Schön
DASS IHR MIT
UNS FEIERT

Tanja

Moodboard 26

WINTER WONDER

PHOTOGRAPHY WEDDINGPILOTS.COM, **WEDDING PLANNING** JAVONHERZEN.DE, **CAKE & SWEET TABLE** SUESS-UND-SALZIG.DE, **FLOWERS** BLUMEN-ROEDER.DE, **WEDDING INVITATIONS** PROJECT-PINPOINT.COM, **HAIR & MAKEUP** ANNIEGOEBEL-MAKEUP.DE, **DJ** SUITE219.DE, **BAND** HUGGEE-SWING.COM, **LOCATION** TRESS-GASTRONOMIE.DE, **FEATURED ON** FRIEDATHERES.COM

Bräutigam
Braut

Macarons
ZITRONE

Angela und Christian
Anfahrt
Menü
SCHÖN, DASS IHR MIT UNS NASCHT
Angela und Christian
Angela und Christian

Moodboard 27
EMERALD ELEGANCE

PHOTOGRAPHY DIANAPLUSVIKI.COM, **FLOWERS** GARDEN EDEN,
HAIR LYDIAGERZEN.DE, **MAKEUP** ANGELIKAPENNER.COM,
BRIDAL FASHION LIGHTANDLACE.DE, **HEADPIECE** LA-CHIA.DE,
WEDDING INVITATIONS ANDREAWOLFDESIGNS.DE, **PRINT** BUTZ-BUERKER.DE,
LOCATION SCHLOSS RAUISCHHOLZHAUSEN, **FEATURED ON** HOCHZEITSWAHN.DE

MONA
MARK
MONA
MARK
MONA
MARK
TISCH
ZWEI
CLARA
MATTHIAS
FELICE
CLEMENS
VIVIENNE
DANIEL
MENÜ
DANKE
DANKE

MONA
MARK

Moodboard 28

HELLO YELLOW

PHOTOGRAPHY POURTOIPHOTOGRAPHIE.COM, **WEDDING PLANNING** JAVONHERZEN.DE, **FLOWERS, DECOR & STYLING** ANMUTUNDSINN.DE, **CAKE** LAGERHAUS-LAUTER.DE, **CAKETOPPER** FRAEULEIN-K-SAGT-JA.DE, **WEDDING INVITATIONS** PROJECT-PINPOINT.COM, **BRIDAL FASHION** BRAUTATELIER-TARA.DE, **HAIR & MAKEUP** STILETT-BOUTIQUE.EU, **MENSWEAR** MRASH.DE, **CEREMONY OFFICIANT** WORTESCHENKEN.DE, **DJ** POM-EVENTS.DE, **MUSIC** JUDITHMUTSCHLER.DE, **LOCATION & CATERING** TRESS-GASTRONOMIE.DE

Mann Frau

Menü
Philipp

Moodboard 29
VERY BERRY

PHOTOGRAPHY JULIABASMANN-PHOTOGRAPHY.DE,
FLOWERS & STYLING BLUETENWERK-BESIGHEIM.DE,
HAIR & MAKEUP PATRICIAKRANICH.DE, **DECOR** GLUECKSSCHAUER.DE,
WEDDING INVITATIONS ANDREAWOLFDESIGNS.DE, **HEADPIECE** JAZZAFINE.DE,
FEATURED IN WEDDINGSTYLE MAGAZINE

Save the Date
Wein
Wein

Moodboard 30

FLOWERS & STRIPES

PHOTOGRAPHY PROJECT-PINPOINT.COM, BETTINA ARNETT **CAKE & SWEET TABLE** PENNYCAKES.DE, **FLOWERS** DIEBLUETE.DE, **WEDDING INVITATIONS** PROJECT-PINPOINT.COM, **HAIR & MAKEUP** MAKE-ME-UP.AT, **MENSWEAR** CINQUE.DE, **WEDDING RING/BRIDE** SCHMUCKGESTALTUNG-EDER.AT, **WEDDING RING/GROOM** BRAND-DESIGN.DE, **GARTER** ETSY.COM, **RENTAL** NIMMPLATZ.COM, **RENTAL/DISHES** ALLESKLAR-VERLEIH.COM, **MUSIC** HANNA-MEYERHOLZ.DE, **CATERING** BLACK-COFFEE-PHARMACY.COM, **FEATURED ON** HOCHZEITSWAHN.DE

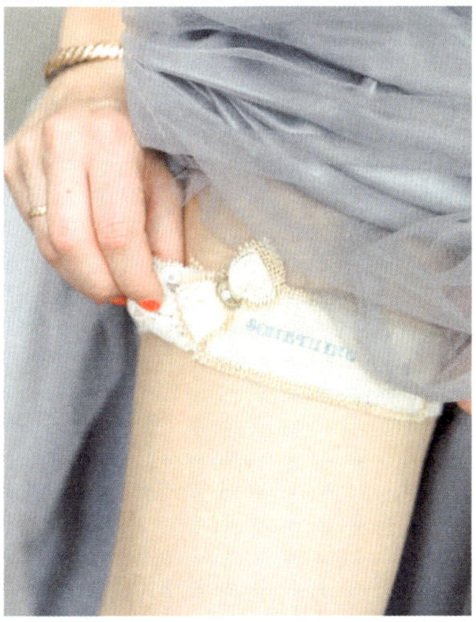

Evi und Michel
28. Mai 2016
Standesamtliche Trauung im Alten Rathaus
Altes Rathaus
Im Anschluss gibt es Kaffee und Kuchen bei uns im Garten.
Wir freuen uns auf euch!
Fam. Hagenlocher | Hochstadenring 7 | 53119 Bonn
Familie Arnett
St. Valentin Strasse 1a
66901 Schönenberg-Kübelberg
Deutschland

Erdnuss
Erdnuss
Erdnuss

Mathes

Moodboard 31

COZY PROVENCE

PHOTOGRAPHY DER-ROTHE-FADEN.DE,
WEDDING INVITATIONS ANDREAWOLFDESIGNS.DE,
HEADPIECES KIDO-DESIGN.DE, **ACCESSORIES** ZURLILAPAMPELMUSE.COM,
BRIDAL FASHION FRAEULEINLIEBE.COM, **HAIR & MAKEUP** JLOOK-MAKEUPART.JIMDO.COM,
FEATURED IN HOCHZEITSWAHN MAGAZINE

Violette
Robert

27.07.15
Violette Robert
BEST DAY
ever
CEREMONY
Cocktails &
DINNER
dancing!
HAPPILY ever
AFTER

Moodboard 32

FREE & WILD

PHOTOGRAPHY LINSE2.AT, **DECOR & STYLING** INALAVIE.COM,
CAKE & SWEETS CAKECOUTURE.AT, **FLOWERS** BLUMENGESTALTEN.AT,
WEDDING INVITATIONS PROJECT-PINPOINT.COM, **BRIDAL FASHION** DASKLEIDSALZBURG.AT,
HAIR & MAKEUP GILBIRD.AT, **VIDEOGRAPHY** SANTIAGO-BOCETA.COM,
LOCATION & DECORATION SUPPLIES WYHNALEK.COM, **MODELS** MAGICMODELS.AT – BETTINA & FABIAN

Menü
AMELIE ♥ BENJAMIN

WIR HEIRATEN
Benjamin

3

Menü

Moodboard 33

LAKE COMO LOVE

PHOTOGRAPHY DAKO-PHOTOGRAPHY.DE, **WEDDING PLANNING & STYLING** STILVOLLES-EVENT.DE, **VIDEOGRAPHY** MARIADITTRICH.COM, **FLOWERS** FIGLIDEIFIORI.COM, **HAIR & MAKEUP** EQUIPEORNELLA.COM, **BRIDAL FASHION** BRAUTMODE-OLENA-KOBLENZ.DE, **MENSWEAR** FEINER-HERR.DE, **RINGS** OHBRACELETBERLIN.DE, **WEDDING INVITATIONS** ANDREAWOLFDESIGNS.DE, **PRINT** BUTZ-BUERKER.DE, **CUPCAKES** LEPOMPOM.DE, **DECOR** OHSOPRETTY.DE, **FAVORS** GLANZGEFUEHL.DE, **LOCATION** VILLAREGINATEODOLINDA.COM & VILLAGENO.IT, **FEATURED ON** WEDDINGCHICKS.COM

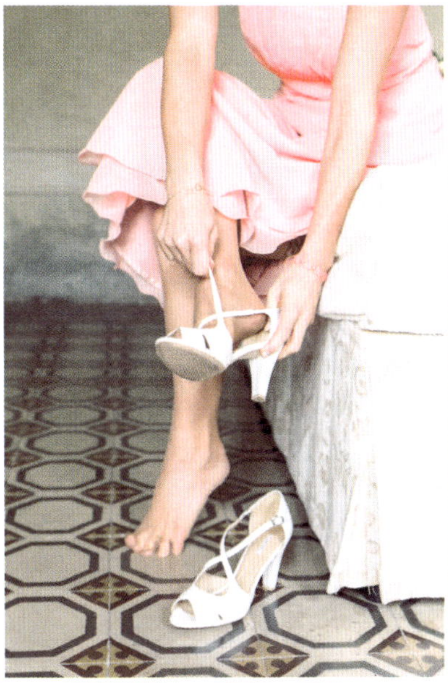

Frédéric

love

Einladung
zu unserer Doppelhochzeit
Invito
al nostro matrimonio doppio
Invitation
for our double wedding

Moodboard 34

ECO LOVERS

PHOTOGRAPHY AGNESUNDANDI.COM, **PLANNING, DECOR & STYLING** HELLBUNT-EVENTS.AT, **CAKE & SWEETS** NOMNOM-V.COM, **FLOWERS** LOK-UNVERBLUEMT.AT, **WEDDING INVITATIONS** PROJECT-PINPOINT.COM, **WEDDING CANDLE** BIO-KERZEN.AT, **BRIDAL FASHION** THERESEUNDLUISE.DE, **HAIR & MAKEUP** DIEHAARGAERTNERIN.AT, **GROOM'S ACCESSORIES** BEWOODEN.DE, **MENSWEAR** BRAINSHIRT.EU & MUSO-KORONI.AT, **WEDDING RINGS** SKREIN.AT, **DECOR RENTAL** NANNA.AT, **LOCATION** ARCHE-NOAH.AT, **MODELS** ANNA & HARALD ZEHETNER, **FEATURED IN** BRAUT MAGAZINE

Danke!

Details
FEIER
WIR LADEN EUCH HERZLICH ZU UNSERER TRAUUNG
AM 22. OKTOBER 2016, UM 14:00 UHR EIN.

Moodboard 35

MALLORCA MOMENTS

PHOTOGRAPHY WOLKEN-MIT-I.COM,
DECOR & STYLING POMPOMYOURLIFE.DE,
WEDDING INVITATIONS ANDREAWOLFDESIGNS.DE,
BRIDAL FASHION HEY-LOVE.DE,
JEWELRY REFINEDBOHEMIA.COM

Moodboard 36
MOODY MAGIC

PHOTOGRAPHY LINSE2.AT, **DECOR & STYLING** INALAVIE.COM,
CAKE & SWEETS TORTENSTUDIO.AT, **FLOWERS** BLUMENGESTALTEN.AT,
WEDDING INVITATIONS PROJECT-PINPOINT.COM, **BRIDAL FASHION** DASKLEIDSALZBURG.AT,
HAIR & MAKEUP GILBIRD.AT, **VIDEOGRAPHY** SANTIAGO-BOCETA.COM,
LOCATION SCHLOSS-WARTHOLZ.AT, **MODELS** ANNA PÖLL & THOMAS PUTZ

Anna & Elias
Elias
Anna
Menü
Anna & Elias
Freuden tränen
Freuden tränen

Süßes

Danke!

Elias
Menü

Moodboard 37

VINTAGE MOOD

PHOTOGRAPHY KATHARINA-WERGEN.DE, **FLOWERS** LILYDELUXE.DE,
MAKEUP SABRINASCHUMACHER.COM, **HAIR** ANNA JOHANNA STEVEN,
BRIDAL FASHION VICTORIARUESCHE.DE, **MENSWEAR** THE-BLOKE.DE,
WEDDING INVITATIONS ANDREAWOLFDESIGNS.DE, **JEWELRY** EMMAKATZKA.COM,
DECOR OHSOVINTAGE.DE, **CAKE & MACAROONS** THE-BAKERS-WIFE.DE, **LOCATION** LA-DUE.DE

I have found the one whom my soul loves

RSVP

Menu

Moodboard 38

FINCA FUN

PHOTOGRAPHY LINSE2.AT, **WEDDING INVITATIONS** PROJECT-PINPOINT.COM,
HAIR & MAKEUP MAKE-ME-UP.AT, **WEDDING RING/BRIDE** SCHMUCKGESTALTUNG-EDER.AT,
WEDDING RING/GROOM BRAND-DESIGN.DE, **BRIDAL FASHION** SHOP.MANGO.COM,
RENTAL/STEREO ENTERTAINMENT-MALLORCA.COM, **BAMBOO PLATES** BIOEINWEGGESCHIRR.DE,
LOCATION FINCALLORCA.DE - FINCA PENITA MALLORCA, **FEATURED IN** BRAUT MAGAZINE

So schön, dass du da bist

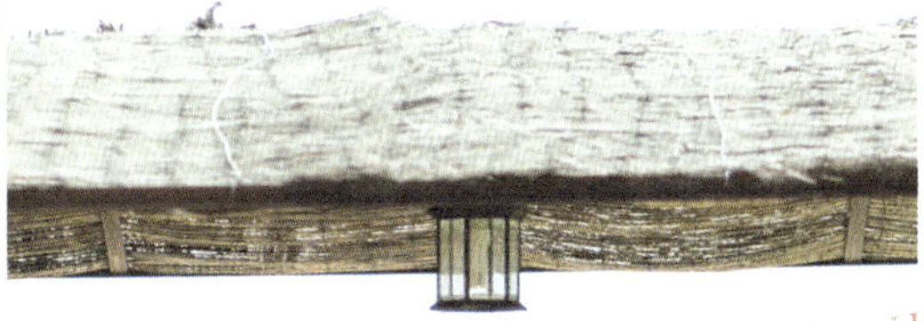

Evi und Michel
Einladung

Moodboard 39

ROMANTIC RIVER

PHOTOGRAPHY KATHLEENJOHN.DE, **WEDDING PLANNING & STYLING** DIEHOCHZEITERIN.COM, **FLOWERS** ASTWERK-AUGSBURG.DE, **HAIR & MAKEUP** VERENA-ROMANTSCHAK.DE, **BRIDAL FASHION** LADONNA-HOCHZEITSATELIER.DE, **RINGS** FINGERGLUECK.DE, **FAVORS** DER-KLEINE-LUXUS.DE, **WEDDING INVITATIONS** ANDREAWOLFDESIGNS.DE, **PRINT** BUTZ-BUERKER.DE, **RENTAL** LANDHAUSGESCHIRR.DE, **COOKIES** MEINKEKSDESIGN.DE, **CAKE** CAKEART STARNBERG, **FEATURED IN** HOCHZEITSWAHN MAGAZINE

Herzliche Einladung
zur Freien Trauung von
Marie-Thérèse König
und
Quirin Xaver Schaber
05. Mai 2016 um 14 Uhr
Wir freuen uns auf Euch!

Moodboard 90

CANDY LAND

PHOTOGRAPHY NADINE-BERNSPITZ-FOTOGRAFIE.DE, **TEAM** HERZENSANGELEGENHEITEN.KOELN, **FLOWERS, DECOR & STYLING** FLORISTIKLOUNGE.COM, **CAKES & SWEETS** PENNYCAKES.DE, **CANDY** KAMELLEBUEDCHEN.DE, **WEDDING INVITATIONS** PROJECT-PINPOINT.COM, **BRIDAL FASHION** GLUECKSGEFUEHL-BRAUTKLEIDER.COM, **HAIR & MAKEUP** SERENA BEVILACQUA, **GROOM'S ACCESSORIES** VONFLOERKE.COM, **WEDDING RINGS** WIRTZ-TRAURINGE.DE, **HANGER & CAKETOPPER** DRAHTLIEBE.COM, **LOCATION** SEE-PAVILLON.DE, **MODELS** THE-MODELS.DE – YANELVIS & RAMJITH, **FEATURED IN** BRAUT MAGAZINE

2
Menü
Einladung

best
day ever

Menü

Groom

Moodboard 41
BOTANICAL FEAST

PHOTOGRAPHY ELENA-ENGELS.DE, **VIDEOGRAPHY** FARINA-KIRMSE.DE,
FLOWERS & STYLING SHABBYCHICEVENTS.DE, **RENTAL** NIMMPLATZ.COM,
BRIDAL FASHION IAM-YOURS.DE, **HAIR & MAKEUP** DOMINIKABRONNER.COM,
WEDDING INVITATIONS ANDREAWOLFDESIGNS.DE, **CAKE** ZARTSUESS.DE, **CATERING** METZGEREI-KLEINJUNG.DE,
MUSIC ERKAN BESIRLIOGLU & JAQUELINE RUBINO, **FEATURED ON** HOCHZEITSWAHN.DE

menu
und
drinks
rsvp
julia
und
gabriel
save
the date

Moodboard 42
FIESTA IN BAVARIA

PHOTOGRAPHY KRISTINA-ASSENOVA.COM, **WEDDING PLANNING, DECOR & STYLING** VERENASOPHIA.DE, **FLOWERS** PETRAMUELLERBLUMEN.DE, **WEDDING INVITATIONS** PROJECT-PINPOINT.COM, **BRIDAL FASHION** FLAMENCO-MUNICH.DE, **HAIR & MAKEUP** VRONI-LIEBL.DE, **WEDDING RINGS** SKUSA-SCHMUCK.DE, **BAND** RAFAELITO-SALSABAND.COM, **PHOTO BOOTH** SUSANNEWYSOCKI.DE, **VIDEOGRAPHY** VISIONONFIRE.CO.ZA, **LOCATION** LAVILLA.DE, **FEATURED IN** MARRYMAG MAGAZINE

Mariana

SAVE THE DATE
AUGUST 1, 2015
VERENA & JAIME
MUNICH | ALEMANIA

1
Elke

Menü
01.08.2015 | VERENA & JAIME
VOM STARNBERGER SEESAIBLING
VON DER STRAUCHTOMATE
RINDERFILETMEDAILLON
DUO VON
Getränke
WEINBEGLEITUNG
BIER
DIGESTIF
ALKOHOLFREIE GETRÄNKE
Kaffee & Tee

Laura
Tisch 8
Christian S.
Tisch 9
Lorena M.
Tisch 2
Susanne W.
Tisch 9
Susan Z.
Tisch 2
Marion B.
Mariana
Elke

Moodboard 43

GREENERY SCENERY

PHOTOGRAPHY SABINELANGE-FOTOGRAFIE.DE & PHOTOLAURICELLA.DE, **FLOWERS** BRAUTSTRAUSS-ATELIER.DE, **DECOR** MITLIEBEZUMDETAIL.INFO, **BRIDAL FASHION** ELBBRAUT.DE, **HAIR & MAKEUP** CAROLIN-GHODOUSSI.DE, **WEDDING INVITATIONS** ANDREAWOLFDESIGNS.DE, **PRINT** BUTZ-BUERKER.DE, **DECOR** TERAMICO.DE, **LOCATION** SPEICHER-WENDIN.DE, **FEATURED ON** MARRYMAG.DE

Save the Date
Infos
Clara & Tom
Antwort
1
Menü

Moodboard 44

RED WINE RENDEZVOUS

PHOTOGRAPHY MARIEBLEYER.COM, **PHOTOGRAPHY ASSISTANT** ANNA-KATHARINA BISCHOF, **PLANNING, DECOR & STYLING** HELLBUNT-EVENTS.AT, **DECOR & STYLING ASSISTANT** SOPHIE FRANK, **CAKE & SWEETS** KUCHENMITSTIL.AT, **FLOWERS** FACEBOOK/STIEL-STÄNGEL, **WEDDING INVITATIONS** PROJECT-PINPOINT.COM, **BRIDAL FASHION** AMBACHERVIDIC.DE, **HAIR & MAKEUP** DIEHAARGAERTNERIN.AT, **WEDDING RINGS** STUDIO-NE.COM, **JEWELRY** ROSAMARLENE.DE, **LOCATION** STADTFLUCHTBERGMUEHLE.AT, **MODELS** HANNA WILD & BERNARDO OLIVEIRA, **FEATURED IN** BRAUT MAGAZINE

Eat me!
OLIVIA & JACOB

SAVE THE DATE
Olivia
and
Jacob
14
03
15
Olivia
Jacob
Eat me!

Moodboard 45

PROVENCIAL PARADISE

PHOTOGRAPHY LUDMILLAPARSYAK-WEDDINGS.COM,
WEDDING PLANNING & STYLING DEL-WEDDINGS.COM,
HAIR & MAKEUP SASKIA-STYLIST.DE, **HEADPIECE** GOLDKNOPF.NET,
WEDDING INVITATIONS ANDREAWOLFDESIGNS.DE, **BRIDAL FASHION** BRAUTZIMMER.COM,
JEWELRY SARAHMIA.DE, **RENTAL** GEHMACHER.AT, **LOCATION** COUVENTDESMINIMES-HOTELSPA.COM

Rsvp

Moodboard 46

IVY WEDDING

PHOTOGRAPHY LINSE2.AT, **PLANNING, DECOR & STYLING** MADEMOISELLE-FEE.AT, **CAKE & SWEETS** KUCHENMITSTIL.AT, **FLOWERS** KARINAVANZINI.COM, **WEDDING INVITATIONS** PROJECT-PINPOINT.COM, **BRIDAL FASHION** MICHELMAYER.AT, **HAIR & MAKEUP** GILBIRD.AT, **WEDDING RINGS** KRAINERSCHMUCK.COM, **RENTAL/DISHES** DIEKAFFEESCHWESTERN.AT, **MODELS** MAGICMODELS.AT, **FEATURED ON** BRAUT.DE

Thank you
Liloé

Vanilla Blackberry

Sweet Menu

Moodboard 47

AUSTRIAN ADVENTURES

PHOTOGRAPHY DAKO-PHOTOGRAPHY.DE, **WEDDING PLANNING, DECOR & STYLING** STILVOLLES-EVENT.DE, **DECOR** LITTLE-PINK-BUTTERFLY.AT, **CAKE** CAKECOUTURE.AT, **FLOWERS** BINDESTELLE.COM, **WEDDING INVITATIONS** PROJECT-PINPOINT.COM, **WOODEN SIGNS** HOLZMITLIEBE.DE, **WEDDING CANDLE** ACRYLMALEREI-SK.AT, **BRIDAL FASHION** DASKLEIDSALZBURG.AT, **HAIR & MAKEUP** JULIA-CHRISTINA.COM, **MENSWEAR** MICSARTORIAL.COM, **JEWELRY & WEDDING RINGS** SCHMUCKGESTALTUNG-EDER.AT, **CEREMONY OFFICIANT** ZUCKERWORTE.COM, **VIDEOGRAPHY** TOM-NENA.COM, **LOCATION** WEISSESROESSL.AT, **MODEL** ELIF & CIHAN SABAH, **FEATURED IN** BRAUT MAGAZINE

Pure Love

Danke
ELISABETH & WOLFGANG

Kirchliche Trauung
ELISABETH & WOLFGANG
Hochzeit
ELISABETH & WOLFGANG
Menü
JOHANN

Moodboard 48

TIFFANY TIME

PHOTOGRAPHY CHRISTINAEDUARD.DE, **WEDDING PLANNING** OLGA-FISCHER.DE, **CAKE & SWEETS** ATELIERSÜSSETRÄUME.DE, **COOKIES** CUPCAKESWORLD.DE, **FLOWERS, DECOR & STYLING** OLGA-FISCHER.DE, **WEDDING INVITATIONS** PROJECT-PINPOINT.COM, **BRIDAL FASHION** WEISS-ZU-SCHWARZ.DE, **HAIR & MAKEUP** NUANCE-HAIRDESIGN.DE, **LOCATION** KOBLENZ-KONGRESS.DE, **MODEL** GIGI JULI

HOCHZEIT
Sabine & Christian
07. JANUAR 2017

Danke

Moodboard 49
SOFT SCRIPT

PHOTOGRAPHY EDELCORNER.AT, **DECOR & STYLING** VENUS-WEDDINGS.COM,
CAKE & SWEETS KATIESCAKES.AT, **CAKE DECORATION** VENUS-WEDDINGS.COM, **FLOWERS** FLORIETTA.AT,
WEDDING INVITATIONS PROJECT-PINPOINT.COM, **BRIDAL FASHION** EDELCORNER.AT – EDELTRAUTSICH,
HAIR & MAKEUP ANDREA-OLEK.AT, **MENSWEAR** STOFFWERK.AT, **JEWELRY** ANTONIA-KOCH.AT,
LOCATION SCHLOSS-WALPERSDORF.NET, **MODELS** JULIA & MANUEL DAX

Valerie
Christian
heiraten
Menü
12 Juli 2017
Valerie

Menü
12 Juli 2017

Moodboard 50
CHRISTMAS CLASSICS

PHOTOGRAPHY CORNELIA-LIETZ.COM, **ORGANISATION** BRIDEMOMENTS.COM,
WEDDING PLANNING TATIANADEWEBER.DE, **FLOWERS** HELENEGUTJAHR.DE,
HAIR & MAKEUP DOMINIKABRONNER.COM, **BRIDAL FASHION** VICTORIARUESCHE.DE,
WEDDING INVITATIONS ANDREAWOLFDESIGNS.DE, **CAKE & SWEETS** ATELIER-GOURMET.COM,
ACCESSORIES SEIDENBAND.COM, **LOCATION** EVENTLOCATION-STELLA-RHENI.DE, **FEATURED IN** BRAUT MAGAZINE

Victoria
und
Benjamin

Sweet
Table

Just
Married

Photography

AGNESUNDANDI.COM

AGNES & ANDI, 2073 PILLERSDORF, AUSTRIA

B-PICTURES.AT

BELINDA PINTER, 9210 POERTSCHACH WOERTHERSEE, AUSTRIA

CHRISTINAEDUARD.DE

CHRISTINA & EDUARD, GRJASIN, 55218 INGELHEIM, GERMANY

CORNELIA-LIETZ.COM

CORNELIA LIETZ, 51515 KUERTEN, GERMANY

DAKO-PHOTOGRAPHY.DE

DANIEL KONDRATIUK, 56179 VALLENDAR, GERMANY

DANIELAMARQUARDT.COM

DANIELA MARQUARDT, 46539 DINSLAKEN, GERMANY

DER-ROTHE-FADEN.COM

KATHRIN ROTH SCHÄDLICH, 97702 MUENNERSTADT, GERMANY

DIANAPLUSVIKI.COM

DIANA & VIKTOR REHAN, 35396 GIESSEN, GERMANY

EDELCORNER.AT

ROLF SCHLADITZ, 2340, MOEDLING, AUSTRIA

ELENA-ENGELS.DE

ELENA ENGELS, 51627 GUMMERSBACH, GERMANY

JULIABASMANN-PHOTOGRAPHY.DE

JULIA BASMANN, 71336 WAIBLINGEN, GERMANY

KATHARINA-WERGEN.DE

KATHARINA WERGEN, 50733 COLOGNE, GERMANY

KATHARINASCHNEE.COM

KATHARINA SCHNEELOCH, 50825 COLOGNE, GERMANY

KATHIUNDCHRIS.DE

KATHI & CHRIS, 44984 BOCHUM, GERMANY

KATHLEENJOHN.DE

KATHLEEN JOHN, 81829 MUNICH, GERMANY

KATJAHEIL.DE

KATJA HEIL, 76344 EGGENSTEIN, GERMANY

KRISTINA-ASSENOVA.COM

KRISTINA ASSENOVA, 81373 MUNICH, GERMANY

LINSE2.AT

DANI & ROLAND VORABERGER, 1150 VIENNA, AUSTRIA

LUDMILLAPARSYAK-WEDDINGS.COM

LUDMILLA PARSYAK, 70569 STUTTGART, GERMANY

MARIEBLEYER.COM

MARIE BLEYER, 1070 VIENNA, AUSTRIA

NADINE-BERNSPITZ-FOTOGRAFIE.DE

NADINE BERNSPITZ, 50259 PULLHEIM, GERMANY

NELLIMAYER.DE

NELLI MAYER, 91625 SCHNELLDORF, GERMANY

NICOLEOTTOPHOTOGRAPHY.DE

NICOLE OTTO, 42651 SOLINGEN, GERMANY

OKTAVIAPLUSKLAUS.COM

OKTAVIA & KLAUS OPPERMANN, 53639 KOENIGSWINTER, GERMANY

PHOTO-LAURICELLA.DE

BEATE LAURICELLA, 51645 GUMMERSBACH, GERMANY

POURTOIPHOTOGRAPHIE.COM

NANA BUDJA, 72793 PFULLINGEN, GERMANY

PROJECT-PINPOINT.COM

BETTINA ARNETT, 36100 VICENZA, ITALY

SABINELANGE-FOTOGRAFIE.DE

SABINE LANGE, 28816 STUHR, GERMANY

SANDRAHUETZEN.DE

SANDRA HÜTZEN, 26441 JEVER, GERMANY

SIEGRIDCAIN.COM

SIEGRID CAIN, 5121 OSTERMIETHING, AUSTRIA

STEFANIENERVERSLEEPS.COM

STEFANIE ROTH, 58540 MEINERZHAGEN, GERMANY

SUSANNEWYSOCKI.DE

SUSANNE WYSOCKI, 80801 MUNICH, GERMANY

WEDDING-YOUANDME.COM

WASSILI JUNGBLUT, 55469 SIMMERN, GERMANY

WEDDINGPILOTS.COM

SUK JAE & JAE IN KIM, 70186 STUTTGART, GERMANY

WOLKEN-MIT-I.COM

LUCAS WILKEN, 45659 RECKLINGHAUSEN, GERMANY

Videography

CASETTI.AT

SIMON CASETTI, 1030 VIENNA, AUSTRIA

FARINAKIRMSE.DE

FARINA KIRMSE, 58511 LUEDENSCHEID, GERMANY

LILAFILM.DE

LISSY SCHUHMANN, 80337 MUNICH, GERMANY

MARIADITTRICH.COM

MARIA DITTRICH, 26831 BUNDE, GERMANY

SANTIAGO-BOCETA.COM

SANTIAGO BOCETA, 1130 VIENNA, AUSTRIA

TOM-NENA.COM

TOM & NENA, 4600 WELS, AUSTRIA

VISIONONFIRE.CO.ZA

IAN BADENHORST, 7915 CAPETOWN, SOUTH AFRICA

Wedding Planning

BRAUTZAUBER.AT

MANUELA WIESER, 9710 FEISTRITZ/DRAU, AUSTRIA

CONAMORE.IT

KATHRIN DOBMANN, 50010 CALDINE, ITALY

DEL-WEDDINGS.COM

DANIELA SCHWARZ, 5020 SALZBURG, AUSTRIA

DIEHOCHZEITERIN.COM

MICHAELA BURCH, 85402 KRANZBERG, GERMANY

FACTSANDFEELINGS.DE

CLAUDIA GEIGER, 51429 BERGISCH GLADBACH, GERMANY

HELLBUNT-EVENTS.AT

TINA HINTERLEITNER, 1020 VIENNA, AUSTRIA

JAVONHERZEN.DE

JACQUELINE DEININGER, 72793 PFULLINGEN, GERMANY

JULIANE BACH

FACEBOOK/JULIANE.DREXLER, 73773 AICHWALD, GERMANY

MADEMOISELLE-FEE.AT

STEFANIE RAUSCH, 1140 VIENNA, AUSTRIA

OLGA-FISCHER.DE

OLGA FISCHER, 55469 SIMMERN/HUNSRUECK, GERMANY

SCHLIPSUNDSCHLEIER.DE

LINDA BREDDEMANN, 57489 DROLSHAGEN, GERMANY

STILVOLLES-EVENT.DE

SINA REINER, 56281 EMMELSHAUSEN, GERMANY

TATIANADEWEBER.DE

TATIANA DE WEBER, 50968 COLOGNE, GERMANY

THE-PERFECT-DAY.AT

SABRINA ULLMANN, 2381 LAAB IM WALDE, AUSTRIA

VENUS-WEDDINGS.COM

RAPHAELA RAMLER, 3100 ST. POELTEN, AUSTRIA

VERENASOPHIA.DE

VERENA SOPHIA BAUER, 81673 MUNICH, GERMANY

WEDS4U.DE

GIORGIA ERLENBUSCH, 71522 BACKNANG, GERMANY

Wedding Invitations

ANDREAWOLFDESIGNS.DE

ANDREA WOLF, 51647 GUMMERSBACH, GERMANY

PROJECT-PINPOINT.COM

EVI HAGENLOCHER, 53119 BONN, GERMANY

BUTZ-BUERKER.DE | PRINT

THOMAS KARCHER, 76135 KARLSRUHE, GERMANY

JEANNETTEMOKOSCH.COM | CALLIGRAPHY

JEANNETTE MOKOSCH, 27344 ROTENBURG WUEMME, GERMANY

Decor & Styling

ACRYLMALEREI-SK.AT | WEDDING CANDLES

SIGRID KIESENHOFER, 4563 MICHELDORF, AUSTRIA

ANMUTUNDSINN.DE

MAREIKE FÖRSTER, 72138 KIRCHENTELLINSFURT, GERMANY

BIO-KERZEN.AT | WEDDING CANDLES

MARTINA NIKOLIĆ, 1070 VIENNA, AUSTRIA

BLÜTENZAUBER

SARAH ERFTKAMP, 42653 SOLINGEN, GERMANY

DEIN-KEKSSTEMPEL.DE

ANDREA SCHWARZ, 73262 REICHENBACH, GERMANY

DEKO-RAUM.AT

BRIGITTE KATZER, 1190 VIENNA, AUSTRIA

DRAHTLIEBE.COM

SHEILIN SHAFIEI, 51065 COLOGNE, GERMANY

FLORISTIKLOUNGE.COM

MARGARETE MIERZWIAK, 50933 COLOGNE, GERMANY

FRAEULEIN-K-SAGT-JA.DE

76344 EGGENSTEIN, GERMANY

GLUECKSSCHAUER.DE

ANDRÉ MATZ, 32351 STEMWEDE, GERMANY

HELLBUNT-EVENTS.AT

TINA HINTERLEITNER, 1020 VIENNA, AUSTRIA

HEYDAY-VIENNA.COM

KATHARINA KIMM, 1150 VIENNA, AUSTRIA

HOLZMITLIEBE.DE

56179 VALLENDAR, GERMANY

INALAVIE.COM

INA TÄUBL, 5020 SALZBURG, AUSTRIA

KÄTHES-LÄDCHEN.AT

KATHRIN HERZOG, 8020 GRAZ, AUSTRIA

LITTLE-PINK-BUTTERFLY.AT

MELANIE SHARMA, 5101 BERGHEIM, AUSTRIA

MADEMOISELLE-FEE.AT

STEFANIE RAUSCH, 1140 VIENNA, AUSTRIA

MELANIE-NOORMANN.DE

MELANIE NOORMANN, 26169 FRIESOYTHE, GERMANY

MITLIEBEZUMDETAIL.INFO

EVA SCHMIDT

OHSOPRETTY.DE

JULIA ALEXA, 50997 COLOGNE, GERMANY

OHSOVINTAGE.DE

JUDITH WALLRAFF, 41469 NEUSS, GERMANY

POMPOMYOURLIFE.DE

MARCELL HUETTNER, 31135 HILDESHEIM, GERMANY

SHABBYCHICEVENTS.DE

MANDY GÖRING, 51674 WIEHL, GERMANY

STIELUNDBLUETE-GRAFENBERG.DE

BETTINA HEMM, 72661 GRANBERG, GERMANY

TERAMICO.DE

LENNART BORN & JEFF IMELMANN, 28832 ACHIM, GERMANY

VENUS-WEDDINGS.COM

RAPHAELA RAMLER, 3100 ST. POELTEN, AUSTRIA

WEDS4U.DE

GIORGIA ERLENBUSCH, 71522 BACKNANG, GERMANY

WYHNALEK.COM

2351 WIENER NEUDORF, AUSTRIA

Flowers

ANMUTUNDSINN.DE

MAREIKE FÖRSTER, 72138 KIRCHENTELLINSFURT, GERMANY

ASTWERK-AUGSBURG.DE

MARION KREILEDER, 86441 ZUSMARSHAUSEN, GERMANY

BINDESTELLE.COM

SANDRA MERHAUT, 5020 SALZBURG, AUSTRIA

BLAUERBAUERNHOF.AT

JULIA STOCKINGER, 3124 OBERWOELBLING, AUSTRIA

BLUETENSTAND.AT

BIRGIT JANCO, 5020 SALZBURG, AUSTRIA

BLUETENWERK-BESIGHEIM.DE

JULIA JANTSCHIK, 74354 BESIGHEIM, GERMANY

BLUMEN-ROEDER.DE

JOHANNES RÖDER, 89077 ULM, GERMANY

BLUMENGESTALTEN.AT

GABRIELE JOCHINGER, 1060 VIENNA, AUSTRIA

BLUMENRAUMGESTALTUNG.COM

ANNA-ELISABETH KRISMER, 1060 VIENNA, AUSTRIA

BLÜTENZAUBER

SARAH ERFTKAMP, 42653 SOLINGEN, GERMANY

BRAUTSTRAUSS-ATELIER.DE

REINER & RALF KORDBARLAG, 28832 ACHIM, GERMANY

CLAUDIAREITINGER.DE

CLAUDIA REITINGER, 86911 DIESSEN, GERMANY

DIE-KATHE.DE

GISELA SPIELVOGEL-KATH, 71717 BEILSTEIN, GERMANY

DIEBLUETE.DE

SABINE SCHEIDTWEILER, 53111 BONN, GERMANY

EVELYNKUEHR.COM

EVELYN KÜHR, 9020 KLAGENFURT, AUSTRIA

FIGLIDEIFIORI.COM

LAURA, 22100 COMO, ITALIA

FLORIETTA.AT

CORNELIA HIERMANN, 3553 SCHILTERN, AUSTRIA

FLORISTIK-HANDWERK.DE

CHRISTIANE KRICHBAUM, 67269 GRUENSTADT, GERMANY

FLORISTIKLOUNGE.COM

MARGARETE MIERZWIAK, 50933 COLOGNE, GERMANY

GARDEN EDEN

KATHARINA NEUFELD, 56566 NEUWIED, GERMANY

GOLDREGEN-FLORALDESIGN.DE

NINA KLEINZ, 50674 COLOGNE, GERMANY

HELENEGUTJAHR.DE

HELENE GUTJAHR, 53913 SWISTTAL MIEL, GERMANY

JARDINDIVERS.IT

50121 FIRENZE, ITALY

KARINAVANZINI.COM

KARIN AVANZINI, 1090 VIENNA, GERMANY

LILYDELUXE.DE

IRIS MÜLLER, 50670 COLOGNE, GERMANY

LOK-UNVERBLUEMT.AT

ANDREJA KUMER, 1050 VIENNA, AUSTRIA

MELANIE-NOORMANN.DE

MELANIE NOORMANN, 26169 FRIESOYTHE, GERMANY

OLGA-FISCHER.DE

OLGA FISCHER, 55469 SIMMERN/HUNSRUECK, GERMANY

PETRAMUELLERBLUMEN.DE

PETRA MÜLLER, 80339 MUNICH, GERMANY

SHABBYCHICEVENTS.DE

MANDY GÖRING, 51674 WIEHL, GERMANY

STIEL-STÄNGEL

FACEBOOK/STIEL-STÄNGEL, 7082 DONNERSKIRCHEN, AUSTRIA

STIELUNDBLUETE-GRAFENBERG.DE

BETTINA HEMM, 72661 GRANBERG, GERMANY

STRAUCHDIEBIN.DE

TINA LANG, 72764 REUTLINGEN, GERMANY

WEDS4U.DE

GIORGIA ERLENBUSCH, 71522 BACKNANG, GERMANY

WELT-DER-ROSALIE.DE

MAJA KLEIN, 82110 GERMERING, GERMANY

Cakes & Catering

ATELIER-GOURMET.COM

MARIA DE FÁTIMA THOMAS, 40667 MEERBUSCH, GERMANY

ATELIERSÜSSETRÄUME.DE

OLGA FUCHS, 55246 MAINZ-KOSTHEIM, GERMANY

BLACK-COFFEE-PHARMACY.COM

53113 BONN, GERMANY

CAKE-SHOP.AT

2325 HIMBERG, AUSTRIA

CAKEART STARNBERG

ANDREA WOISCH, 82319 STARNBERG, GERMANY

CAKECOUTURE.AT

ANDREA STREITWIESER, 5020 SALZBURG, AUSTRIA

CAKESTYLING.DE

ALEKSANDRA MATIJAŞEVIC, 70180 STUTTGART, GERMANY

CUPCAKESWORLD.DE

JULIA BAERWALD, 97422 SCHWEINFURT, GERMANY

DIECUPCAKERY.DE

SANDRA BETTENHAUSEN, 51766 ENGELSKIRCHEN, GERMANY

GRETARMARLENE.DE

JASMIN WEISS, 42657 SOLINGEN, GERMANY

KAMELLEBUEDCHEN.DE

50667 COLOGNE, GERMANY

KATIESCAKES.AT

KATHARINA SANTIN, 2500 BADEN, AUSTRIA

KUCHENMITSTIL.AT

DAGMAR PAUSER, 7035 STEINBRUNN, AUSTRIA

LAGERHAUS-LAUTER.DE

RUTH LAEPPLE, 72532 GOMADINGEN-DAPFEN, GERMANY

LEPOMPOM.DE

PANTEHA JAMALPOUR, 50674 COLOGNE, GERMANY

MADAMEMIAMMIAM.DE

ANNE SCHULTES-SCHMITZ, 51067 COLOGNE, GERMANY

MASTERCLASS-CAKE.DE

DIMITRI ECKERT, 55469 SIMMERN, GERMANY

MEINKEKSDESIGN.DE

STEPHANIE JULIETTE RINNER, 80339 MUNICH, GERMANY

NOMNOM-V.COM

MELANIE KRÖPFL, 1020 VIENNA, AUSTRIA

PENNYCAKES.DE

SABRINA ZEHNPFENNIG, 50933 COLOGNE, GERMANY

RICHTIG-SUESS.DE

REBECCA SCHWEIZER, 79117 FREIBURG, GERMANY

SUESS-UND-SALZIG.DE

HEIKE KROHZ, 73079 SUESSEN, GERMANY

SUGARBIRD-CUPCAKES.DE

ANNETTE ROSA MARQUES, 40237 DUSSELDORF, GERMANY

THE-BAKERS-WIFE.DE

MARIE AND GEORG LABUDE, 40219 DUSSELDORF, GERMANY

TORTENSTUDIO.AT

ANDREA KARGL, 1230 VIENNA, AUSTRIA

TRESS-GASTRONOMIE.DE

DANIEL TRESS, 72534 HAYINGEN, GERMANY

WHISKYANDMORE.COM

OLIVER BEIROW, 19055 SCHWERIN, GERMANY

WIRMACHENCUPCAKES.COM

CHRISSIE LOUBSER, 80469 MUNICH, GERMANY

ZARTSUESS.DE

ANNEMARIE SUTORIS, 51674 WIEHL, GERMANY

Hair & Makeup

ANDREA-OLEK.AT

ANDREA KÖBERL, 3143 PYHRA, AUSTRIA

ANGELIKAPENNER.COM

ANGELIKA PENNER, 56269 DIERSDORF, GERMANY

ANNA JOHANNA STEVEN

ANNA JOHANNA STEVEN, 51149 COLOGNE, GERMANY

ANNIEGOEBEL-MAKEUP.DE

ANNIE GOEBEL, 70439 STUTTGART, GERMANY

ARMILLABEAUTY.COM

MAURO, 50022 GREVE IN CHIANTI, ITALY

CAROLIN-GHODOUSSI.DE

CAROLIN GHODOUSSI, GERMANY

DESIREE-RENAUD.DE

DESIREE RENAUD, 83684 TEGERNSEE, GERMANY

DIEHAARGAERTNERIN.AT

LELA, 1140 VIENNA, AUSTRIA

DOMINIKABRONNER.COM

DOMINIKA BRONNER, PITTSBURGH, USA

EQUIPEORNELLA.COM

ORNELLA, 22100 COMO, ITALIA

ALEXANDRA CONDOPOULOS

FACEBOOK/A.CONDOPOULOS, 1090 VIENNA, AUSTRIA

FEENGLEICH-MAKEUP.COM

CARINA BAUER-UNZEITIG, 1090 VIENNA, AUSTRIA

GILBIRD.AT

CLAUDIA FROMASCHITZ, 1130 VIENNA, AUSTRIA

JLOOK-MAKEUPART.JIMDO.COM

JENNIFER SANDER, 29342 WIENHAUSEN, GERMANY

JULIA-CHRISTINA.COM

JULIA CHRISTINA WEISS,

83483 BISCHOFSWIESEN, GERMANY

KRISTINA AILEEN ROSSKAMP

KRISTINA AILEEN ROSSKAMP, 26689 APEN, GERMANY

LA-CHIA.DE

CHIARA NIGGELOH, 58285 GEVELSBERG, GERMANY

LONA-STYLING.DE

NATA, 70180 STUTTGART, GERMANY

LYDIAGERZEN.DE

LYDIA GEZEN, 56271 MAROTH, GERMANY

MAKE-ME-UP.AT

ANGELA HUBMANN, 5020 SALZBURG, AUSTRIA

MASKENRAUM.DE

CHRISTINA NEUSS, 50678 COLOGNE, GERMANY

MUSITOWSKI.COM

CARINA MUSITOWSKI, 40235 DUSSELDORF, GERMANY

NUANCE-HAIRDESIGN.DE

LARISA MAHALOVA, 60314 FRANKFURT, GERMANY

PATRICIAKRANICH.DE

PATRICIA KRANICH, 74376 GEMMRIGHEIM, GERMANY

SABRINASCHUMACHER.COM

SABRINA SCHUMACHER, 40235 DUSSELDORF, GERMANY

SASKIA-STYLIST.DE

SASKIA MÜLLER, 73728 ESSLINGEN, GERMANY

SCHMINKRAUM.COM

SILKE JESKE, 76646 BRUCHSAL, GERMANY

STILETT-BOUTIQUE.EU

GINA WEIDENT-IGNATZI, 72764 REUTLINGEN, GERMANY

VERENA-ROMANTSCHAK.DE

VERENA ROMANTSCHAK,

85411 HOHENKAMMER, GERMANY

SERENA BEVILACQUA

FACEBOOK/SERENA BEVILACQUA, COLOGNE, GERMANY

VRONI-LIEBL.DE

VERONIKA LIEBL, 85560 EBERSBERG, GERMANY

WEDDINGSTYLE BY CICEK

51643 GUMMERSBACH, GERMANY

Bridal Fashion

123BRAUT.COM
68519 VIERNHEIM, GERMANY
AMBACHERVIDIC.DE
20359 HAMBURG, GERMANY
BRAUTATELIER-TARA.DE
70178 STUTTGART, GERMANY
BRAUTMODE-OLENA-KOBLENZ.DE
56077 KOBLENZ, GERMANY
BRAUTZIMMER.COM
5020 SALZBURG, AUSTRIA
DASKLEIDSALZBURG.AT
MARLENE SCHEIBER,
5020 SALZBURG, AUSTRIA
EDELCORNER.AT
CLAUDIA SCHLADITZ, 2340 MOEDLING, AUSTRIA
ELBBRAUT.DE
THERESA STEINKE,
20459 HAMBURG, GERMANY
EVASCHOLZ.COM
EVA SCHOLZ, 50676 COLOGNE, GERMANY
FLAMENCO-MUNICH.DE
80802 MUNICH, GERMANY
FRAEULEINLIEBE.COM
39104 MAGDEBURG, GERMANY
FREIWILD-DESIGN.AT
3340 WAIDHOFEN/YBBS, AUSTRIA
GLUECKSGEFUEHL-BRAUTKLEIDER.COM
50226 FRECHEN, GERMANY
HEY-LOVE.DE
80538 MUNICH, GERMANY
HEYDAY-VIENNA.COM
1150 VIENNA, AUSTRIA
IAM-YOURS.DE
40237 DUSSELDORF, GERMANY
KISUI.DE
10585 BERLIN, GERMANY
LADONNA-HOCHZEITSATELIER.DE
84069 SCHIERLING, GERMANY
LIGHTANDLACE.DE
33647 BIELEFELD, GERMANY
MICHELMAYER.AT
MICHEL MAYER, 1010 VIENNA, AUSTRIA
NONI-MODE.DE
50825 COLOGNE, GERMANY
SALONDIVA.SK
81106 BRATISLAVA, SLOVENIA
SARAHMIA.DE
72070 TUEBINGEN, GERMANY
SINAFISCHERDESIGN.DE
SINA FISCHER, 72461 ALBSTADT, GERMANY
SINAFISCHERDESIGN.DE
72461 ALBSTADT, GERMANY
THERESEUNDLUISE.DE
83512 WASSERBURG/INN, GERMANY
TIANVANTASTIQUE.COM
86923 FINNING, GERMANY
VICTORIARUESCHE.DE
50676 COLOGNE, GERMANY
WEISS-ZU-SCHWARZ.DE
61440 OBERURSEL, GERMANY

Accessories

EDITAROSENROT.COM
EDITA ROSENROT, 1090 VIENNA, AUSTRIA
GOLDKNOPF.NET
70173 STUTTGART, GERMANY
JANNIEBALTZER.COM
JANNIE BALTZER, 2300 COPENHAGEN, DENMARK
JAZZAFINE.DE
CAROLINE BEJENAR, 69517 GORXHEIMERTAL, GERMANY
KIDO-DESIGN.DE
KIRSTIN DORDAN, 85579 NEUBIBERG, GERMANY
LA-CHIA.DE
CHIARA HIGGELOH, 58285 GEVELSBERG, GERMANY
SCHUHNIQUE.DE
MONIKA MAIER, 83236 UEBERSEE, GERMANY
SEIDENBAND.COM
TANJA KIBOGO, 53721 SIEGBURG, GERMANY
WIESN-TASCHERL.DE
DAGMAR SASSADECK, 83123 AMERANG, GERMANY
ZURLILAPAMPELMUSE.COM
NADINE VILLMANN, 51467 BERGISCH GLADBACH, GERMANY

Rings & Jewelry

ANTONIA-KOCH.AT
ANTONIA KOCH, 3131 WALPERSDORF, AUSTRIA
BKING.DE
BERNADETT KING, 94227 ZWIESEL, GERMANY
BRAND-DESIGN.DE
JOHANNES BRAND, 53111 BONN, GERMANY
EDITAROSENROT.COM
EDITA ROSENROT, 1090 VIENNA, AUSTRIA
EMMAKATZKA.COM
EMMA KATZKA, CHARLESTON, USA

FINGERGLUECK.DE

IRIS MERKLE, 70176 STUTTGART, GERMANY

KRAINERSCHMUCK.COM

ELISABETH KRAINER, 1010 VIENNA, AUSTRIA

LA-CHIA.DE

CHIARA NIGGELOH, 58285 GEVELSBERG, GERMANY

OHBRACELETBERLIN.DE

MARIE GALINSKY SCHILD, 10997 BERLIN, GERMANY

REFINEDBOHEMIA.COM

JESSICA SCHÄFER, 57250 NETPHEN, GERMANY

ROSAMARLENE.DE

ROSA MARLENE, 1080 VIENNA, AUSTRIA

SARAHMIA.DE

SARAH KNÖLLER, 72070 TUEBINGEN, GERMANY

SCHMUCKGESTALTUNG-EDER.AT

ALEXANDRA EDER, 5120 ST. PANTALEON, AUSTRIA

SKREIN.AT

1010 VIENNA, AUSTRIA

SKUSA-SCHMUCK.DE

JUDITH LORENZ, 80469 MUNICH, GERMANY

STUDIO-NE.COM

NICOLE EITEL, 70174 STUTTGART, GERMANY

TRAGKULTUR.DE

IMKE VAN DER VOORT, 40479 DUSSELDORF, GERMANY

WIRTZ-TRAURINGE.DE

53111 BONN, GERMANY

MUSO-KORONI.AT

1080 VIENNA, AUSTRIA

STOFFWERK.AT

1010 VIENNA, AUSTRIA

STRODELUNDJAEGER.DE

58511 LUEDENSCHEID, GERMANY

THE-BLOKE.DE

40477 DUSSELDORF, GERMANY

VONFLOERKE.COM

53111 BONN, GERMANY

WHITEMONKEY.DESIGN

85049 INGOLSTADT, GERMANY

XUITS.DE

60322 FRANKFURT, GERMANY

Favors & Gifts

DER-KLEINE-LUXUS.DE

BRITTA HAERTEL, 67583 GUNTERSBLUM, GERMANY

GLANZGEFUEHL.DE

TINA KARTEN, 41189 MOENCHENGLADBACH, GERMANY

SCHOENERTAGNOCH.BLOGSPOT.IT

JULIANE HALLER, 76448 DURMERSHEIM, GERMANY

Menswear

BEWOODEN.DE

61118 BAD VILBEL, GERMANY

BRAINSHIRT.EU

36043 FULDA, GERMANY

CINQUE.DE

41066 MOENCHENGLADBACH, GERMANY

FEINER-HERR.DE

50733 COLOGNE, GERMANY

FREIWILD-DESIGN.AT

3340 WAIDHOFEN AN DER YBBS, AUSTRIA

HERRENBUDE.DE

50823 COLOGNE, GERMANY

HERRVONEDEN.COM

20357 HAMBURG, GERMANY

MICSARTORIAL.COM

56073 KOBLENZ, GERMANY

MONSIEUR-AGNES.DE

50674 COLOGNE, GERMANY

MRASH.DE

70197 STUTTGART, GERMANY

Rentals

ALLESKLAR-VERLEIH.COM

50996 COLOGNE, GERMANY

ALLESKLAR-VERLEIH.COM

5081 ANIF, AUSTRIA

DIEKAFFEESCHWESTERN.AT

BRIGITTE WEINZIERL, 1060 VIENNA, GERMANY

ENTERTAINMENT-MALLORCA.COM

MARK HINTERSCHEID, 07609 LLUCMAJOR, SPAIN

GEHMACHER.AT

5020 SALZBURG, AUSTRIA

LANDHAUSGESCHIRR.DE

79822 TITISEE-NEUSTADT, GERMANY

LIESCHENUNDRUTH.DE

ELLA METZ, 33335 GUETERSLOH, GERMANY

NANNA.AT

1060 VIENNA, AUSTRIA

NIMMPLATZ.COM

50670 COLOGNE, GERMANY

NOLEGGIOCHIANTI500.IT

53011 CASTELLINA IN CHIANTI, ITALY

Ceremony Officiants

ANGELIKA SCHÖN | TEXTE & GEDICHTE

FACEBOOK/SCHOENERGEIST, 5020 SALZBURG, AUSTRIA

DIEHOCHZEITERIN.COM

MICHAELA BURCH, 85402 KRANZBERG, GERMANY

DIETRAUUNG.DE

ANNE-KATRIN GEHRING, 42897 REMSCHEID, GERMANY

GLUECKSVERBREITER.DE

CHRISTINANE SCHIVELBEIN, 26209 HATTEN, GERMANY

JEANNINE-GEBAUER.DE

JEANNINE GEBAUER, 53773 HENNEF, GERMANY

WORTESCHENKEN.DE

GABRIELE A. SCHMIDT, 72793 PFULLINGEN, GERMANY

ZUCKERWORTE.COM

KRISTINA WENDNER, AUSTRIA

Music

JUDITHMUTSCHLER.DE

JUDITH MUTSCHLER, 88367 HOHENTENGEN/BREMEN, GERMANY

HANNA-MEYERHOLZ.DE

HANNA MEYERHOLZ, 48145 MUENSTER, GERMANY

NEOMARKS.DE

NEO MARKS, 50496 COLOGNE, GERMANY

HUGGEE-SWING.COM

JOACHIM HARRES, 10999 BERLIN, GERMANY

NEUTON.DE

ANNA & TOBIAS, 50825 COLOGNE, GERMANY

POM-EVENTS.DE

CHRISTIAN BACHMANN, 73110 HATTENHOFEN, GERMANY

RAFAELITO-SALSABAND.COM

RAFAEL PAREJA, 80637 MUNICH, GERMANY

SUITE219.DE

TILL SEIZER, 73249 WERNAU, GERMANY

Locations

ARCHE-NOAH.AT

PAVILLON IM ARCHE NOAH SCHAUGARTEN,
3553 SCHILTERN, AUSTRIA

BLACK-COFFEE-PHARMACY.COM

53113 BONN, GERMANY

COUVENTDESMINIMES-HOTELSPA.COM

HOTEL COUVENT DES MINIMES,
04300 MANE-EN-PROVENCE, FRANCE

DESIGNOFFICES.DE | STUTTGART-MITTE

DESIGNOFFICE STUTTGART, 70173 STUTTGART, GERMANY

DIETRAEUMEREI.AT

DIE TRÄUMEREI, 8382 WEICHSELBAUM, AUSTRIA

DOCKONE.DE

NEW YORKER DOCK ONE, 51063 COLOGNE, GERMANY

EVENTLOCATION-STELLA-RHENI.DE

VILLA STELLA RHENI, 53177 BONN, GERMANY

FINCALLORCA.DE

FINCA PENITA, 07530 SANT LLORENC, MALLORCA, SPAIN

GOURMETBERNER.DE

GOURMET BERNER, 71384 WEINSTADT, GERMANY

GRAFENEGG.COM

SCHLOSS GRAFENEGG, 3485 GRAFENEGG, AUSTRIA

HOTEL-AHE.DE

GUT AHE, 57399 KIRCHHUNDEM, GERMANY

KOBLENZ-KONGRESS.DE

KURFÜRSTLICHES SCHLOSS, 56068 KOBLENZ, GERMANY

LA-DUE.DE

LA DÜ, 40549 DUSSELDORF, GERMANY

LAVILLA.DE

LA VILLA, 82343 NIEDERPOECKING, GERMANY

MANGIACANE.COM

VILLA MANGIACANE, 50026 FLORENCE, ITALY

PALAISLIECHTENSTEIN.COM

PALAIS LIECHTENSTEIN, 1090 VIENNA, AUSTRIA

SCHLOSS-WALPERSDORF.NET

SCHLOSS WALPERSDORF, 3131 WALPERSDORF, AUSTRIA

SCHLOSS-WARTHOLZ.AT

SCHLOSS WARTHOLZ, 2651 REICHENAU/RAX, AUSTRIA

SCHLOSSHOTEL-DIERSFORDT.DE

SCHLOSS DIERSFORDT, 46487 DIERSFORDT, GERMANY

SEE-PAVILLON.DE

SEE PAVILLION, 50769 COLOGNE, GERMANY

SKITERRASSEN.DE

HOOKSIELER SKITERRASSEN, 26434 HOOKSIEL, GERMANY

SPEICHER-WENSIN.DE

GUT WENSIN, 23827 WENSIN, GERMANY

STADTFLUCHTBERGMUEHLE.AT

STADTFLUCHT BERGMUEHLE, 2123 KRONBERG, AUSTRIA

STRUDLHOF.AT

HOTEL & PALAIS STRUDLHOF, 1090 VIENNA, AUSTRIA

TRESS-GASTRONOMIE.DE

SCHLOSS EHRENFELS, 72534 HAYINGEN, GERMANY

VILLAGENO.IT

VILLA GENO, 22100 COMO, ITALY

VILLAREGINATEODOLINDA.COM

VILLA REGINA TEODOLINDA, 22010 COMO, ITALY

VON-WINNING.DE

WEINGUT VON WINNING, 67146 DEIDESHEIM, GERMANY

WEISSESROESSL.AT

WEISSES RÖSSL, 5360 ST. WOLFGANG, AUSTRIA

Blogs & Magazines

BRAUT.DE
BRAUTMAGAZIN.DE
BRIDEMOMENTS.DE
FRAEULEIN-K-SAGT-JA.DE
FRIEDATHERES.COM
HOCHZEITSGUIDE.DE
HOCHZEITSWAHN.DE
MARRYMAG.DE
THE-LITTLE-WEDDING-CORNER.DE
WEDDINGCHICKS.COM
WEDDINGSTYLE.DE

PHOTO OCTAVIAPLUSKLAUS.COM

GET INSPIRED

www.colormoodboards.com

facebook.com/colormoodboards

instagram.com/colormoodboards